Editor in Chief
Ina Massler Levin, M.A.

Cover Designer
Karen J. Goldfluss, M.S. Ed.

Cover Artist
Marilyn Goldberg

Creative Director
Karen J. Goldfluss, M.S. Ed.

Imaging
Rosa C. See

CD Credits
Application Programmer
Charles Payne

Graphics Design
David Kiefer

Publisher

Mary D. Smith, M.S. Ed.

Interactive L[...]

for **All INTERACTIVE**

Daily Sentence Editing

CORRELATED TO **COMMON CORE** STANDARDS

Factories   vehicles   two
~~factorys~~ and motor ~~vehicals~~ are ~~too~~

main sources   air pollution
of the ~~mane~~ ~~sorces~~ of ~~err~~ pollution.

* Developed for **ALL** Interactive Whiteboards
* Hundreds of ready-to-edit sentences to practice and review grammar, punctuation, and spelling
* Includes Standards and Benchmarks

Teacher Created Resources

Author
Eric Migliaccio

Teacher Created Resources
12621 Western Avenue
Garden Grove, CA 92841
www.teachercreated.com

ISBN: 978-1-4206-3886-8

©2010 Teacher Created Resources
Reprinted, 2019
Made in U.S.A.

Teacher Created Resources

Table of Contents

Introduction

Imagine a classroom tool that could make grammar and spelling interesting and involving for your students, a tool that could get your entire class excited and engaged in learning proper punctuation. *Daily Sentence Editing* is a program that has been designed to do all of this and more. Compatible with all interactive whiteboards, *Daily Sentence Editing* offers the many advantages of touchscreen technology and allows your students to participate in learning like never before.

Each *Daily Sentence Editing* CD comes pre-loaded with the entire slate of sentences from the accompanying book. The book contains 30 units worth of sentences, allowing you to teach one unit per week, if desired. New grammar rules are incorporated into each of the first 15 units. In this way, grammar, punctuation, and spelling concepts are introduced and then reinforced in a systematic manner, allowing students to practice each concept before learning a new one. The final 15 units of each book and CD offer a cumulative reinforcement of all of the rules and concepts learned.

These sentences can be accessed and printed from the CD or copied from the book. They can be done as in-class work or assigned as homework. Corrections to these sentences can then be made on individual computers or on an interactive whiteboard in front of the class. All it takes is a finger or a special pen, depending on the interactive board you use. You and your students can correct the sentences in several ways:

☞ by writing and drawing directly onto the interactive whiteboard

☞ by grabbing punctuation stamps built into the program and dragging them over the corresponding errors

☞ by switching to typewriter mode and retyping the sentence correctly on the screen.

An intuitive array of buttons and menus allows you to do (and undo) every correction quickly and easily and in six custom colors. Best of all, it takes just one quick click of a button for teachers and students to see the correct answers. And as an added teaching tool, another touch of a button will show students the locations of the sentence's errors without revealing the actual answers.

In addition to the sentences that come pre-loaded on the CD, the *Daily Sentence Editing* program allows you to create and save thousands of custom sentences or paragraphs. With one time-saving touch of a button, the program can even make incorrect versions of your custom creations by adding punctuation and capitalization errors for you. An "Instant Sentence" function allows sentences and paragraphs of up to 200 characters in length to be made instantly, giving even greater in-class flexibility. Teachers can use this tool to tap into their class's creativity with student-generated sentences and peer-editing exercises.

Best of all, installation is a snap. In no time, you will have the power of interactive learning at your students' fingertips . . . and yours.

About the CD

The real flexibility and interactivity of the *Daily Sentence Editing* program shines through in the resources included on the CD.

☞ Install the CD

Just pop the CD that accompanies this book into your PC or Mac, and you and your students can begin editing sentences at individual computers or on the interactive white board in your classroom. (**Quick Tip:** If needed, step-by-step installation instructions are provided on the inside front cover of this book.)

☞ The Main Menu

Once you have installed the CD, the Main Menu will appear on your computer screen or interactive white board. (**Quick Tip:** The Main Menu will open up in full-screen mode. If you wish to resize the Main Menu screen, hit the ESC button. This will allow you to adjust it as needed.)

From the Main Menu, you can access all of the features and resources available in the program. To get a detailed explanation of these features, click on the Guide button. This will take you to the *Daily Sentence Editing* User's Guide.

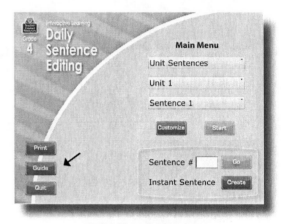

Main Menu Screen

☞ The User's Guide

Everything you need to know in order to use and operate the *Daily Sentence Editing* CD and program can be found in the User's Guide. This is also where you will find useful reproducibles that you may wish to hand out to your students. These include . . .

- a one-page handout of the editing symbols used in the program. These marks are available as punctuation stamps on the editing screen for each sentence.

- a one-page overview for each of the 30 units in the book. Each overview includes a list of the grammar rules and concepts that are introduced in the unit, as well as a list of the rules reviewed in the unit. A complete list of the ready-to-be edited sentences in the unit is also included here.

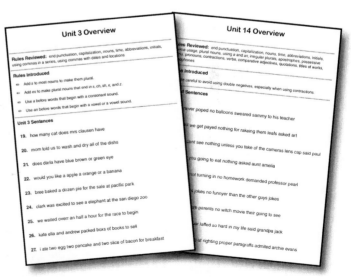

About the CD *(cont.)*

The User's Guide on the CD contains a lot of important and helpful information. However, you may wish to immediately begin editing and/or creating sentences with your students. The following Quick-Start Guides will help you do just that.

Quick-Start Guide for Editing Sentences

1. **Launch the Program:** Load the CD and launch the program. If needed, follow the installation instructions on the inside front cover of this book.

2. **Click the Start Button:** You can access the **Start** button from the **Main Menu** screen. (See the graphic to the right.) This will take you directly to the editing screen. (See the graphic at the bottom of the page.)

3. **Edit the Sentences:** Write, draw, or paint directly onto the screen. You may also use the punctuation stamps located on either side of the screen. Grab, drag, and drop these stamps onto, above, or below the sentence to correct the errors.

4. **Check Your Work:** Click on the **Show Errors** button to give your students hints about where the errors can be found in the sentence. Click on the **Show Correct** button to reveal the correct version of the sentence.

5. **Edit a New Sentence:** Click on the **Next** button to continue the editing lesson with a new sentence.

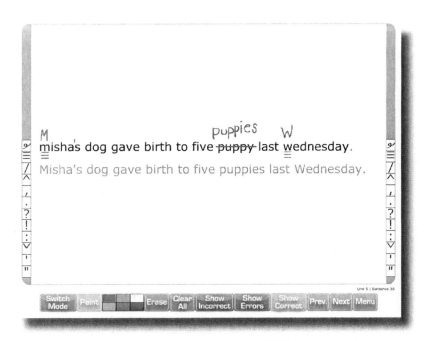

About the Book

There are two main components to the *Daily Sentence Editing* program: a book and a CD. These two parts were designed to be complementary, but they can also be used independently of one another.

This 112-page book is a good place to begin the program. It contains the following:

☞ **Tips for Using the CD** (pages 5–6)

The following two pages include tips for getting started with the CD that accompanies this book.

☞ **Common Core State Standards** (page 7)

The grammar rules and concepts reviewed in this book meet the Common Core State Standards.

☞ **Grammar Rules** (pages 8–12)

This book includes a comprehensive list of the punctuation, capitalization, and usage rules students will need to know in order to correct the sentences. New rules are introduced in each of the first 15 units, allowing students to learn increasingly difficult grammar concepts at a measured pace, while reviewing the ones they have previously learned. The final 15 units serve as a cumulative review of the rules learned in the first 15 units.

☞ **Ready-To-Be-Edited Sentences** (pages 13–102)

In all, there are 270 sentences, each of which contains multiple errors. These sentences are divided into 30 units, which allows you to teach one unit's worth of sentences per week, if desired. Each sentence in the book is followed by plenty of space for your students to rewrite the sentence correctly. These pages can be copied and used as in-class assignments or sent home as homework.

☞ **Answer Key** (pages 103–112)

A complete answer key is included at the back of the book. This key contains the corrected versions of all 270 sentences found in the book.

(**Quick Tip:** Each answer in the key represents the best or most-likely correction of the sentence. In some instances, however, there may be alternate ways in which to correct a sentence. Please accept suitable responses when comparing student answers to the key.)

Meeting Standards

The activities in this book meet one or more of the following Common Core State Standards. © Copyright 2010. National Governors Association Center for Best Practices and Council of Chief State School Officers. All rights reserved. For more information about the Common Core State Standards, go to *http://www.corestandards.org/*.

Reading Standards: Foundational Skills

Fluency

4. Read with sufficient accuracy and fluency to support comprehension.
   - Read grade-level text with purpose and understanding.
   - Use context to confirm or self-correct word recognition and understanding, rereading as necessary.

Language Standards

Conventions of Standard English

1. Demonstrate command of the conventions of standard English grammar and usage when writing or speaking.
   - Form and use the progressive verb tenses.
   - Produce complete sentences, recognizing and correcting inappropriate fragments and run-ons.
   - Correctly use frequently confused words.

2. Demonstrate command of the conventions of standard English capitalization, punctuation, and spelling when writing.
   - Use correct capitalization.
   - Use commas and quotation marks to mark direct speech and quotations from a text.
   - Use a comma before a coordinating conjunction in a compound sentence.
   - Spell grade-appropriate words correctly, consulting references as needed.

Grammar Rules

The following pages include most of the grammar, usage, and punctuation rules students will need to know to edit the sentences in this book. The units in which these rules are applicable are listed in parentheses after each rule.

Rule 1: A *sentence* is a group of words that tells a complete thought. Capitalize the first word in a sentence. A *statement* is a sentence that tells something. Put a period at the end of a telling sentence. A *question* is a sentence that asks something. Put a question mark at the end of an asking sentence. An *exclamation* is a sentence that shows feeling. It ends with an exclamation mark. A *command* is a sentence that tells someone to do something. It ends with a period or an exclamation mark. **(Units 1–30)**

- **My dog is black.**
- **Do you have a pet?**
- **We won the game!**
- **Please print your name.**
- **Get out of the street!**

Rule 2: Capitalize the word "I." **(Units 1–30)**

- **Scott and I are friends.**

Rule 3: *Nouns* are words that name people, places, things, and ideas. **(Units 1–30)**

- **The doctor sat in his office.**
- **Honesty is the best policy.**

Rule 4: *Proper nouns* name specific people, places, and things. Proper nouns begin with a capital letter. *Common nouns* are not specific. Common nouns do not begin with a capital letter. **(Units 1–30)**

- **Jane saw a magician named Gregor the Great.**
- **The Johnsons went to New York to see the Statue of Liberty.**

Rule 5: A *colon* is used between the hour and minutes when writing the time of day. **(Units 1–30)**

- **We went to school at 8:00.**

Rule 6: An *abbreviation* is a short form of a word. Capitalize name titles and put a period after ones that have been shortened into an abbreviation. Also capitalize and put a period after initials, which are letters used instead of a full name. **(Units 1–30)**

- **The shop is owned by Mr. Payne.**
- **My dentist is Dr. Anna Lee.**
- **The author of the book is J.P. Wilson.**

Rule 7: Capitalize the days of the week, months of the year, and holidays. Do not capitalize seasons of the year. **(Units 1–30)**

- **Is Memorial Day on a Monday in May?**
- **My favorite season is spring.**

Grammar Rules *(cont.)*

Rule 8: Use a *comma* to separate the day and year or to separate the day and month. Use a comma to separate a city and state or country. **(Units 2–30)**

- **She was born on Thursday, November 2, 2006, in Houston, Texas.**
- **We went to the beach, ate lunch, and saw a movie on Saturday.**

Rule 9: A series is a list of three or more items. Use a comma to separate three or more words or groups of words in a series. **(Units 2–30)**

- **Would you rather have pizza, pasta, or a hamburger?**

Rule 10: A *singular noun* names one person, place, thing, idea, or animal. A *plural noun* names more than one person, place, thing, idea, or animal. Add *s* to most nouns to make them plural. Add *es* to words that end in *s, ch, sh, x,* and *z.* **(Units 3–30)**

- **I have two small <u>dogs</u> and one big <u>dog</u>.**
- **I see one blue <u>dish</u> and two red <u>dishes</u>.**

Rule 11: Use *a* or *an* before singular nouns. Use *a* before words that begin with a consonant sound. Use *an* before words that begin with a vowel or vowel sound. **(Units 3–30)**

- **He ate <u>a</u> piece of toast and <u>an</u> egg <u>an</u> hour before school began.**

Rule 12: Nouns that end in the letter *y* have special rules for making plurals. If the word ends with a vowel followed by *y*, just add *s*. If the word ends with a consonant followed by *y*, change the *y* to *i* and add *es*. **(Units 4–30)**

- **Dad put his <u>keys</u> in his coat pocket.**
- **I went to three birthday <u>parties</u> in June.**

Rule 13: Nouns that end is *f* or *fe* also have a special rule for making plurals. In most words, change the *f* to *v* and add *es*. **(Units 4–30)**

- **I found six butter knives and one bread knife in the drawer.**

Rule 14: A *possessive noun* shows ownership. Use an *apostrophe* and an *s* (*'s*) after a noun to show that something belongs to one person or thing. To form the plural possessive of a plural noun that ends in *s*, add only an apostrophe. If the plural noun does not end in *s*, add an apostrophe and an *s*. **(Units 5–30)**

- **<u>Beth's</u> guitar is sitting next to <u>Jess's</u> drum set.**
- **Both of his <u>brothers'</u> bikes are blue.**
- **We visited the <u>children's</u> library yesterday.**

Rule 15: A *pronoun* is a word that is used in place of a noun. Use the pronouns *I* and *me* correctly. Use the pronoun *I* when you are doing something. Use the pronoun *me* when something happens to you. **(Units 6–30)**

- **Mom and <u>I</u> went to Hawaii.**
- **She waved to Bob and <u>me</u>.**

Grammar Rules _(cont.)_

Rule 16: Use the personal pronouns _we/us, she/he, her/him,_ and _they/them_ correctly. Also use possessive pronouns (e.g., _mine, ours, his, hers, its, theirs_) correctly. Use "we" when you and others are doing something. Use "she/he/they" when a person or group is doing something. Use "us" when something happens to you and others. Use "her/him/them" when something is happening to a person or a group. **(Units 6–30)**

- **<u>We</u> went to school.**
- **<u>He</u> is riding the bike.**
- **Sam gave <u>him</u> a ride.**
- **That house is <u>ours</u>.**

- **<u>They</u> gave the trophy to us.**
- **<u>She</u> will cook dinner for them.**
- **Bill took <u>her</u> to the movie.**
- **Is this book <u>yours</u>?**

Rule 17: A _contraction_ is a word made by joining two words. When joining the words, a letter or letters are left out. An apostrophe is put in the word at the spot where the letter or letters are missing. **(Units 7–30)**

- **We are going home.**
- **She did not see him.**
- **He will be there soon.**

- **<u>We're</u> going home.**
- **She <u>didn't</u> see him.**
- **<u>He'll</u> be there soon.**

Rule 18: A name can be made into a contraction, as well as a possessive by adding _'s._ The _'s_ can mean "is" or "has," depending on the sentence. **(Units 7–30)**

- **<u>Mary's</u> going to Canada this summer.** _(contraction for "is")_
- **<u>Mary's</u> been packing for her trip.** _(contraction for "has")_
- **I saw <u>Mary's</u> car parked in the lot.** _(possessive)_

Rule 19: The _verb_ often shows the action of the sentence. When the subject of the sentence is singular, an _s_ or _es_ is usually added to the verb (except with the pronouns _I_ or _you_.) When the subject is plural, an _s_ is not added to the verb. **(Units 8–30)**

- **Ryan <u>eats</u> a lot of food. Eric and Bob <u>eat</u> more food. I <u>eat</u> the most.**
- **The school <u>fixes</u> lunch for us. They <u>fix</u> lunch for us everyday.**

Rule 20: The verbs _am, are, is, was,_ and _were_ are forms of the word _be._ They are not action words. Instead, they tell what someone or something is like. **(Units 8–30)**

Use "am" with the word "I."

Use "is" and "are" when talking about what is happening now.

Use "was" and "were" when talking about things that have already happened.

Use "is" and "was" when talking about one person, place, thing, idea, or animal.

Use "are" and "were" when talking about more than one person, place, thing, idea, or animal and with the word "you."

- **I <u>am</u> six year old. You <u>are</u> older than I am.**
- **Jim <u>is</u> seven years old. Last year, Jim <u>was</u> six.**
- **Kate and Nate <u>are</u> eight. They <u>were</u> seven last year.**

Grammar Rules *(cont.)*

Rule 21: A *present-tense verb* shows action that happens now. A *past-tense verb* tells about an action that already happened. Add *ed* to most verbs to form the past tense. In addition to *s* and *es*, the ending *ing* can also be added to present-tense verbs. If the verb has a single vowel and ends with a consonant, the last consonant is usually doubled before adding *ed* or *ing*. If the word ends with a silent *e*, drop the final *e* before adding *ed* or *ing*. **(Units 8–30)**

- **The car <u>stops</u> here now. It also <u>stopped</u> here yesterday. Will it be <u>stopping</u> here every day?**
- **I <u>wave</u> goodbye. I <u>waved</u> to everybody. I am <u>waving</u> my hand.**

Rule 22: If a verb ends with a consonant and *y*, change the *y* to *i* and add *es* to form the present-tense verb. If a verb ends with a consonant and *y*, change the *y* to *i* and add *ed* to form a past-tense verb. **(Units 8–30)**

- **Each team <u>tries</u> to win.**
- **I <u>tried</u> to hit a home run.**

Rule 23: The past tense of some verbs is made by changing the spelling. **(Units 8–30)**

- **Last week my dog <u>ran</u> away.** *(run)*
- **He <u>bought</u> some milk at the store.** *(buy)*
- **He <u>drew</u> a picture in art class.** *(draw)*

Rule 24: Helping verbs are sometimes used with main action verbs. Some examples of helping verbs are *has, have, had, is, are, was, were,* and *will*. **(Units 8–30)**

- **Yesterday I <u>saw</u> you at the mall. I <u>have seen</u> you there before.**

Rule 25: An *adjective* is a word that describes a noun or a pronoun. Add *er* to most adjectives to compare two people, places, things, etc. Add *est* to compare more than two. **(Units 9–30)**

- **Lee is <u>taller</u> than Joe. In fact, Lee is the <u>tallest</u> student in the class.**

Rule 26: Commas are used to separate some elements in a sentence. **(Units 10–30)**

Use a comma after "yes" or "no" at the beginning of a sentence.

- **<u>Yes,</u> I am going to the store. <u>No,</u> you are not.**

Use a comma to separate introductory words or phrases at the beginning of a sentence.

- **<u>Wow,</u> it's hot today! <u>Well,</u> it was hotter yesterday.**
- **<u>If I remember correctly,</u> it was cold and rainy last week.**

Use a comma to set off the name of a person being directly addressed or described.

- **<u>Bill,</u> are you going to the party? Yes, <u>Tim,</u> I am.**

Use a comma to set off the word *too* when meaning "also."

- **I want to go to the movies, <u>too</u>. That, <u>too,</u> can be done.**

Grammar Rules *(cont.)*

Rule 27: A *quotation* shows a speaker's exact words. Use *quotation marks* at the beginning and ending of a quotation to show where the speakers started and stopped talking. Begin a quotation with a capital letter. In a *telling* sentence, use a comma between the quotation and the rest of the sentence. **(Units 11–30)**

- Sal said, "We are going to the zoo."
- "We are going to the zoo," said Sal.

Rule 28: In an *asking* sentence, use a question mark after the quotation. If the quotation is before the speaker's name, put a period at the end of the sentence. If the speaker's name is before the quotation, separate the quotation with a comma. The same rules apply in an *exclamation*. **(Units 11–30)**

- Lily asked, "Can I go with you?"
- "Can I go with you?" asked Lily.
- "That house is on fire!" shouted Al.
- Al shouted, "That house is on fire!"

Rule 29: When writing the title of a book, movie, play, newspaper, music collection, or television show, underline the entire title and capitalize the first word, the last word, and each important word. Follow the same capitalization rules but use quotation marks around the titles of stories, poems, and songs. **(Units 12–30)**

- We read the book Holes in class.
- We heard "Somewhere Over the Rainbow" from The Wizard of Oz.

Rule 30: A *homophone* is a word that sounds the same as another word but has a different spelling or meaning. Be careful not to confuse these and other misused words, such as *are/our* and *it's/its.* **(Units 13–30)**

- I can see the ship out on the sea.
- Scott ate eight donuts for breakfast!
- Are you coming to our house today?
- It's time to give the dog its bath.

Rule 31: A *negative* is a word like *no, not, none,* or *never.* A contraction with the word *not* is also a negative. Do not use two negatives together in a sentence. **(Units 14–30)**

- She never had ~~no~~ lunch.
- Can't you see ~~nothing~~?
- She never had any lunch.
- Can't you see anything?

Rule 32: A *run-on sentence* has two complete thoughts that run into each other. If the ideas in the two parts are separate thoughts, divide them into two sentences with a period. If the two ideas have something in common, add a comma and a *conjunction* (a connecting word such as *and, but, so,* or *yet*) to form a *compound sentence.* **(Units 15–30)**

- They go to East School their favorite subject is math. *(incorrect)*
- They go to East School, and their favorite subject is math. *(correct)*
- Pablo wanted to play ball he couldn't find the field. *(incorrect)*
- Pablo wanted to play ball, but he couldn't find the field. *(correct)*

susan and i saw a Movie on friday at 730

Unit 1
Sentence 1

_____

_____

_____

mr hill has taught at grant high school for 15 years

Unit 1
Sentence 2

_____

_____

_____

have you been to the grand canyon in arizona

Unit 1
Sentence 3

_____

_____

_____

those dancers are amazing

Unit 1
Sentence 4

_____

_____

_____

his best friend is named a j johnson

Unit 1
Sentence 5

_____

_____

_____

the warners spent the Winter near whistler mountain in canada

Unit 1
Sentence 6

_____

_____

_____

Name: _____   Date: _____

our plane will depart from oklahoma city at 945 am

Unit 1
Sentence 7

_____

_____

_____

is your spanish teacher named mrs cordova

Unit 1
Sentence 8

_____

_____

_____

angie asked if memorial day is in april or may

Unit 1
Sentence 9

_____

_____

_____

Name: _____ Date: _____

sara cindy and michelle are going to africa on
may 12 2012

Unit 2
Sentence
10

_____

_____

_____

mr miller flew to miami florida for a business meeting

Unit 2
Sentence
11

_____

_____

_____

tito has an appointment with dr stone on monday june 5

Unit 2
Sentence
12

_____

_____

_____

tanya grows peppers tomatoes and squash in her garden

Unit **2**

Sentence **13**

_____

_____

_____

joey was born in cleveland ohio on august 19 2004

Unit **2**

Sentence **14**

_____

_____

_____

mrs alualu said that it is 400 a m in hilo hawaii right now

Unit **2**

Sentence **15**

_____

_____

_____

mark and i played soccer baseball and tennis this sumer

Unit 2
Sentence 16

_____

_____

_____

the olsens bought the house at 368 main st on april 12 2007

Unit 2
Sentence 17

_____

_____

_____

should i take a train plane or boat from london england to paris france

Unit 2
Sentence 18

_____

_____

_____

how many cat does mrs clausen have

Unit 3
Sentence 19

_____

_____

_____

mom told us to wash and dry all of the dishs

Unit 3
Sentence 20

_____

_____

_____

does darla have blue brown or green eye

Unit 3
Sentence 21

_____

_____

_____

would you like a apple a orange or a banana

Unit 3
Sentence 22

_____

_____

_____

bree baked a dozen pie for the sale at pacific park

Unit 3
Sentence 23

_____

_____

_____

clark was excited to see a elephant at the san diego zoo

Unit 3
Sentence 24

_____

_____

_____

we waited overr an half a hour for the race to begin

Unit 3
Sentence 25

_____

_____

_____

kate ella and andrew packed boxs of books to sell

Unit 3
Sentence 26

_____

_____

_____

i ate two egg two pancake and two slice of bacon for breakfast

Unit 3
Sentence 27

_____

_____

_____

did you know that an hundred pennys equal one dollar

Unit 4
Sentence
28

_____

_____

_____

i think those two puppys look like little wolfs

Unit 4
Sentence
29

_____

_____

_____

amy bought two hat two scarf and one pair of glove

Unit 4
Sentence
30

_____

_____

_____

there are the same number of day in august july and may

Unit 4
Sentence 31

_____

_____

_____

is it true that craig and sue are both having partys on saturday

Unit 4
Sentence 32

_____

_____

_____

the great wall of china is one of the most famuss landmark in asia

Unit 4
Sentence 33

_____

_____

_____

did delia and deeann dress as witchs on halloween

Unit 4

Sentence 34

_____

_____

_____

felicia and her family visited eight beachs this summer

Unit 4

Sentence 35

_____

_____

_____

we bought two cream pie six pastry and a dozen cookie at boston bakery

Unit 4

Sentence 36

_____

_____

_____

mias three brothers are named martin max and maurice

Unit **5**
Sentence **37**

_____

_____

_____

is it true that mrs basss new glasses are brite yellow

Unit **5**
Sentence **38**

_____

_____

_____

**arturos baseball team scored nine run in the
fourth inning**

Unit **5**
Sentence **39**

_____

_____

_____

her two brothers wifes are both named alice

Unit 5
Sentence
40

_____

_____

_____

all of the childrens parent's watched the game
and cheered

Unit 5
Sentence
41

_____

_____

_____

charles' chores were to clean the birds cage and
the fishs tank

Unit 5
Sentence
42

_____

_____

_____

walter walks wandas two dog's every monday morning at 915

Unit **5**

Sentence **43**

_____

_____

_____

mr tanner taught us that rome is the name of italys capital city

Unit **5**

Sentence **44**

_____

_____

_____

peters parents names are paul and penelope parsons

Unit **5**

Sentence **45**

_____

_____

_____

him is the new teacher at kennedy junior high school

Unit 6
Sentence
46

_____

_____

_____

annies uncle gave she a new bike for christmas

Unit 6
Sentence
47

_____

_____

_____

are them going to jill jones house for thanksgiving dinner

Unit 6
Sentence
48

_____

_____

_____

~~~~~~

her watched jimmy and i play two tennis match

Unit **6**
Sentence **49**

_____

_____

_____

~~~~~~

dee and me have been freinds since november 11 2007

Unit **6**
Sentence **50**

_____

_____

_____

~~~~~~

us are going to wrigley field to watch the chicago cubs play

Unit **6**
Sentence **51**

_____

_____

_____

p j and her are the two best student in mr teals class

Unit 6
Sentence 52

my brother my sister and me all have brown eye's

Unit 6
Sentence 53

martha made two pan of brownie for they and i

Unit 6
Sentence 54

hes going to turn 10 year old on september 2 2012

Unit 7
Sentence 55

_____

_____

_____

im the best spellerr in mrs thomas'es class

Unit 7
Sentence 56

_____

_____

_____

mrs fords the principal at pine bluff elementary school

Unit 7
Sentence 57

_____

_____

_____

ill tell mom and dad that youll be late for diner

Unit 7

Sentence 58

_____

_____

_____

ive earnned twenty more dollar than ricks earned

Unit 7

Sentence 59

_____

_____

_____

did'nt you see sal cindy and steve at westlake mall

Unit 7

Sentence 60

_____

_____

_____

is earths biggest body of watter the pacific ocean

Unit **7**

Sentence **61**

_____

_____

_____

mom said you shouldnt eat the soop if its too hot

Unit **7**

Sentence **62**

_____

_____

_____

president franklin d roosevelts first yeer in office
was 1933

Unit **7**

Sentence **63**

_____

_____

_____

tommy and me runs faster than leah and josh

Unit 8

Sentence 64

_____

_____

_____

we was the ones who pickd up all you trash yesterday

Unit 8

Sentence 65

_____

_____

_____

well be driveing thru arizona new mexico and texas this summer

Unit 8

Sentence 66

_____

_____

_____

Name: _____ Date: _____

~~~~~~

them leaved for school at about 700 a m tooday

_____

_____

_____

~~~~~~

mr martin maked us sit in our chairs for a hour after class

_____

_____

_____

~~~~~~

cassie cryed out when the movies hero falled into the lions cage

_____

_____

_____

Name: _____ Date: _____

trevors team stoped at food mart to buy drink and snack

Unit 8
Sentence 70

_____

_____

_____

is we sleepping over at aunt debs house tomorrow night

Unit 8
Sentence 71

_____

_____

_____

the wilson's payed p j and i to watch their house while theyre in iowa

Unit 8
Sentence 72

_____

_____

_____

Name: _____ Date: _____

those is the bigest butterflys i've ever seen

_____

_____

_____

i heared that the weather will be much hoter tommorow

_____

_____

_____

is tina tam the smarter person in mrs birchs entire class

_____

_____

_____

claudia and me buyed heavyer blankets for the winter

Unit 9
Sentence
76

_____

_____

_____

do fewest people live in india china or the united states

Unit 9
Sentence
77

_____

_____

_____

the judge sayed that kevins cookies was the
tastyer of them all

Unit 9
Sentence
78

_____

_____

_____

Name: _____ Date: _____

**i has been the talllest one of my freinds since
the third grade**

_____

_____

_____

**them's the funnyest guys in the town of
blue ridge virginia**

_____

_____

_____

**her was the happyest one in the house when
her team winned**

_____

_____

_____

mrs mackey may i sharpen me pencil now

_____

_____

_____

no andre you cant play until you finnish your homework

_____

_____

_____

wow those puppys are the tinyest and furryest
things ever

_____

_____

_____

yes we was the ones who goed to the concert last night

Unit 10
Sentence 85

_____

_____

_____

mom who eated the cupcake i leaved on the kitchen tabel

Unit 10
Sentence 86

_____

_____

_____

is him on the oakview high school boys
volleyball team too

Unit 10
Sentence 87

_____

_____

_____

i too seen the firefighter save mrs clearys cat

Unit 10
Sentence
88

_____

_____

_____

will you be leting us leave erly today mr timmons

Unit 10
Sentence
89

_____

_____

_____

yes uncle nate is the older of the seven mans in his family

Unit 10
Sentence
90

_____

_____

_____

Name: _____ Date: _____

yes ill go if youre going too said alexander

Unit 11

Sentence 91

_____

_____

_____

dont tuch that hot oven yeled mrs anderson

Unit 11

Sentence 92

_____

_____

_____

whos the curent mayor of our town asked mr fitz

Unit 11

Sentence 93

_____

_____

_____

is them the thiefs who robed the bank asked officer kline

Unit 11

Sentence
94

_____

_____

_____

bobby sayed no you cant borrow my brothers bicycle

Unit 11

Sentence
95

_____

_____

_____

eli exclaimd wow thats the goodest burger ive ever eaten

Unit 11

Sentence
96

_____

_____

_____

~~~~~~

oops gasped vince after tiping over mrs vances
valuable vase

Unit 11
Sentence
97

_____

_____

_____

~~~~~~

ollie asked is ottawa ontario or quebec the capital
of canada

Unit 11
Sentence
98

_____

_____

_____

~~~~~~

pam pointed at a fin comeing out of the oshun
and screamed shark

Unit 11
Sentence
99

_____

_____

_____

lilys little sister watched finding nemo five times this summer

Unit 12

Sentence 100

_____

_____

_____

dr david singed us a song called a apple a day

Unit 12

Sentence 101

_____

_____

_____

donalds dad asked have you readed charlottes web by e b white

Unit 12

Sentence 102

_____

_____

_____

clarissas cousins favorite film is beauty and the beast

Unit 12

Sentence 103

_____

_____

_____

did dolly realy watch six episode of "dora the explorer" today

Unit 12

Sentence 104

_____

_____

_____

is it true that aunt sues favorite song is twist and shout by the beatles

Unit 12

Sentence 105

_____

_____

_____

shood we watch eragon star wars or shrek asked alejandro

Unit 12
Sentence 106

_____

_____

_____

kims class read the lion the witch and the wardrobe by c s lewis

Unit 12
Sentence 107

_____

_____

_____

mia thinked that flowers was the best poem in the book spring poetry

Unit 12
Sentence 108

_____

_____

_____

carls cousin craig catched the bawl and throwed it back to carl

Unit 13

Sentence 109

_____

_____

_____

im so hungry said harry as he eight a hole pepperoni pizza

Unit 13

Sentence 110

_____

_____

_____

how many loafs of bread will we need to make fourty sandwitches

Unit 13

Sentence 111

_____

_____

_____

cant you sea the atlantic ocean from hear asked nancy

Unit 13
Sentence 112

_____

_____

_____

gabriella gived up and said its know use

Unit 13
Sentence 113

_____

_____

_____

lous sister asked who's blew shoos are those
in lous room

Unit 13
Sentence 114

_____

_____

_____

are friend frank is the gratest guitar player in
kern county

Unit 13

Sentence
115

_____

_____

_____

two of the mane grains growed in spain is wheat
and barley

Unit 13

Sentence
116

_____

_____

_____

wally telled the waiter id like a eg and two peaces
of toast please

Unit 13

Sentence
117

_____

_____

_____

Name: _____   Date: _____

Unit 14
Sentence
118

i never poped no balloons sweared sammy to his teacher

_____

_____

_____

Unit 14
Sentence
119

dont we get payed nothing for rakeing them leafs asked art

_____

_____

_____

Unit 14
Sentence
120

you cant see nothing unless you take of the cameras lens cap said paul

_____

_____

_____

~~~~~~

are'nt you going to eat nothing asked aunt amelia

Unit 14

Sentence
121

_____

_____

_____

~~~~~~

**whose not turning in no homework demanded
professor pearl**

Unit 14

Sentence
122

_____

_____

_____

~~~~~~

wasn't his jokes no funnyer than the other guys jokes

Unit 14

Sentence
123

_____

_____

_____

doesnt there parents no witch movie their going to see

Unit 14
Sentence 124

_____

_____

_____

i havent never laffed so hard in my life said grandpa jack

Unit 14
Sentence 125

_____

_____

_____

i aint no good at righting proper paragraffs admited archie evans

Unit 14
Sentence 126

_____

_____

_____

jenny spyed on shirley she finded out the good news that way

Unit 15
Sentence 127

_____

_____

_____

todd wanted to serf there weren't no waves at the beech today

Unit 15
Sentence 128

_____

_____

_____

tims parents drived to the supermarket they buyed sum grocerys

Unit 15
Sentence 129

_____

_____

_____

charles maked a whole in the yard he buryed the treasure their

Unit 15

Sentence 130

_____

_____

_____

we tryed to sat through the hole boreing movie we could'nt

Unit 15

Sentence 131

_____

_____

_____

dont play with matchs never leave a candle burning said fireman rick

Unit 15

Sentence 132

_____

_____

_____

we didnt find no wind so we couldnt fly are kites

Unit 15
Sentence 133

_____

_____

_____

we seen fore movies yesterday we liked only too of them

Unit 15
Sentence 134

_____

_____

_____

rex and me maked paper airplains we flyed them
all day long

Unit 15
Sentence 135

_____

_____

_____

kay like to eat onion ring but she nose there not good for her

Unit **16**
Sentence **136**

_____

_____

_____

titus bot a brush a komb and some hare jell at super mart

Unit **16**
Sentence **137**

_____

_____

_____

do anyone no whose goeing to visit henry at the Hospital

Unit **16**
Sentence **138**

_____

_____

_____

ouch cryed bonnie when she was stinged by a be

Unit 16
Sentence
139

_____

_____

_____

they went to logan beach they swimmed for an our

Unit 16
Sentence
140

_____

_____

_____

the two childs said mommy we want to see a
elephunt at the zoo

Unit 16
Sentence
141

_____

_____

_____

the grizzly bare standed up in the rivver on it's hind leggs

Unit 16
Sentence 142

_____

_____

_____

annabel said the goodest gifts come in littel boxs

Unit 16
Sentence 143

_____

_____

_____

trent needed too new tire and a pare of windshield wippers for his car

Unit 16
Sentence 144

_____

_____

_____

would you like a lollipop asked lucy yes i wood said stan

Unit **17**

Sentence **145**

_____

_____

_____

dad joged to hansen park mom and me rided
are bikes there

Unit **17**

Sentence **146**

_____

_____

_____

ty asked can i borow two dollers i dont have no money
replyed mary

Unit **17**

Sentence **147**

_____

_____

_____

the wite rabbitt hoped over the small fents to get into the garden

Unit 17
Sentence 148

whos bean siting in me chair asked papa bear

Unit 17
Sentence 149

the two mans were in charge of garding the queens jewls

Unit 17
Sentence 150

Name: _____ Date: _____

mr archer angryly asked who's car is parkt in my space

Unit 17
Sentence
151

_____

_____

_____

weave seen rein snow and sleet this weak whats
next asked ed

Unit 17
Sentence
152

_____

_____

_____

the princess sleeped on a pilow made from the fethers
of golden gooses

Unit 17
Sentence
153

_____

_____

_____

ostrichs is the heavyest birds they can way over 300 pounds

Unit 18
Sentence 154

_____

_____

_____

the tinyest bird meazures only 2.2 inchs long its a humingbird

Unit 18
Sentence 155

_____

_____

_____

did you know that an horse can live twise as many yeers as a squirel

Unit 18
Sentence 156

_____

_____

_____

~~~~~~

a female dear is called a doe a mail deer is called a stag

Unit 18

Sentence
157

_____

_____

_____

~~~~~~

a tigers babys are called cubs a bares are too

Unit 18

Sentence
158

_____

_____

_____

~~~~~~

wow it wood take a snale about 30 ours to crawl won mile

Unit 18

Sentence
159

_____

_____

_____

a tarantula is a harry spyder it can live for fiffteen year

Unit 18
Sentence 160

_____

_____

_____

turtels alligaters and lizerds is all reptiles frogs arent

Unit 18
Sentence 161

_____

_____

_____

some african elephants can gro to be twelv foots tall thats huge

Unit 18
Sentence 162

_____

_____

_____

dr martin luther king, jr was awardded the
nobel peace prize in 1964

Unit 19
Sentence
163

_____

_____

_____

yellowstone national park in wyoming is home to
bears wolfs and deers

Unit 19
Sentence
164

_____

_____

_____

in 1927 charles lindbergh becomed the first to
fly ackross the atlantic ocean alone

Unit 19
Sentence
165

_____

_____

_____

yankee doodle is the offishal state song of connecticut

Unit 19

Sentence 166

_____

_____

_____

the only working dimond mine in north america is in arkansas

Unit 19

Sentence 167

_____

_____

_____

neil named all 50 u s state capitals nick forgetted that idahos is boise

Unit 19

Sentence 168

_____

_____

_____

delaware oficially becoming the first u s state
on december 7 1787

Unit 19
Sentence 169

_____

_____

_____

california arizona and oklahoma is the states where
the most native americans live today

Unit 19
Sentence 170

_____

_____

_____

the worlds largest ball of twine can be finded in
kansas it weigh over 18,000 pounds

Unit 19
Sentence 171

_____

_____

_____

jupiter and saturn are the too bigest plants in are soler system

Unit 20
Sentence 172

_____

_____

_____

the galaxy we live in is calld the milky way it contanes bilions of star

Unit 20
Sentence 173

_____

_____

_____

the planet venus is maid up mostly of rock while neptune is mayed mostly of gass

Unit 20
Sentence 174

_____

_____

_____

there are a belt of rocks called asteroids beetween mars and joopiter

Unit 20
Sentence 175

_____

_____

_____

a comet is a moveing chunk of ice dust and rock in space

Unit 20
Sentence 176

_____

_____

_____

the moon make no lite of it's own it reflect lite from the son

Unit 20
Sentence 177

_____

_____

_____

it take just over 365 daze for earth to revolve
around the sunn thats one year

Unit 20
Sentence
178

_____

_____

_____

the first humen to orbit earth was yuri gagarin him
did this on april 12 1961

Unit 20
Sentence
179

_____

_____

_____

on july 20 1969 neil armstrong becomed the first
to wok on the moon

Unit 20
Sentence
180

_____

_____

_____

a penny equals one sent a nickle equal five scents

Unit 21
Sentence
181

_____

_____

_____

paper monney was most likelly inventted in china

Unit 21
Sentence
182

_____

_____

_____

the country of fiji use wales' tooths as money
until about 100 year ago

Unit 21
Sentence
183

_____

_____

_____

do you know whose on the american $100 bill
its benjamin franklin

Unit 21
Sentence
184

_____

_____

_____

ben franklin was a politican a righter a inventor
and a sientist

Unit 21
Sentence
185

_____

_____

_____

he inventted the lightning rod, witch helps to keeps
bildings safe from lightening

Unit 21
Sentence
186

_____

_____

_____

our science teacher mr quail asked me what
cawses lightning

Unit 21

Sentence
187

_____

_____

_____

the blizard maked driveing on the towns rodes
allmost imposible

Unit 21

Sentence
188

_____

_____

_____

a hurricain warning is isshued when their are winds
over 74 miles per our

Unit 21

Sentence
189

_____

_____

_____

we learnt in helth class about food eksercise and
the parts of are bodys

Unit 22
Sentence 190

_____

_____

_____

the digestive sistem brakes food down and mooves
it threw your body

Unit 22
Sentence 191

_____

_____

_____

you was born with 350 bones some have growed
toogether now you have 206

Unit 22
Sentence 192

_____

_____

_____

are the five senses hearing site smell taste
and tuch asked serena

Unit 22
Sentence
193

_____

_____

_____

wite blood sells in are body help us to fite viruses
and bacteria

Unit 22
Sentence
194

_____

_____

_____

the cerebrum is the part off the brane that control
thinkking speach and vizion

Unit 22
Sentence
195

_____

_____

_____

water is verry importent it help us grow dijest food
and get rid of waists

Unit 22
Sentence
196

_____

_____

_____

we has three leg bone theyr'e the femur the tibia
and the fibula

Unit 22
Sentence
197

_____

_____

_____

andy asked does joging burrn more calorees then
swiming

Unit 22
Sentence
198

_____

_____

_____

Name: _____ Date: _____

a fotographer speaked to are class yester day
her camera was incredible

_____

_____

_____

the three primery colorrs is red blew and yelow
said are art teacher mrs han

_____

_____

_____

them went on a feeled trip to the j paul getty museum
in los angeles

_____

_____

_____

is it troo that this billding was desined by your uncle asked avery

Unit 23
Sentence 202

carl axsed the hotel manajer hey why dont this plase have a 13th floor

Unit 23
Sentence 203

the first elevater was install in a new york store in 1857 it was powered by steem

Unit 23
Sentence 204

the worlds most long bridge over water is in louisiana
its all most 24 miles long

Unit 23
Sentence
205

_____

_____

_____

witch explorer is the hudson bay named after mr alt
asked erin

Unit 23
Sentence
206

_____

_____

_____

wow we spended the morning hikeing on a byootiful
path called lizzys trail

Unit 23
Sentence
207

_____

_____

_____

the dryest areas on earth is desserts the wetest are rein forrests

Unit 24
Sentence 208

abowt 67 persent of our worlds surfuss is coverred wit ocean water

Unit 24
Sentence 209

australias great barrier reef is earths larggest coral reaf

Unit 24
Sentence 210

Name: _____ Date: _____

solar powwer use energee that come direckly
from sunlite

Unit 24

Sentence
211

_____

_____

_____

the ozone layer protecks us from the suns raze it is
hi above earth

Unit 24

Sentence
212

_____

_____

_____

factorys and motor vehicals are too of the mane sorces
of err polution

Unit 24

Sentence
213

_____

_____

_____

we shood take our emptee soda cans to the recycleing senter today

Unit 24
Sentence 214

_____

_____

_____

does those companys use recycled paper too make there sereal boxxes

Unit 24
Sentence 215

_____

_____

_____

mayer jones is asking four our help in cleening the cities beachs this saturday

Unit 24
Sentence 216

_____

_____

_____

the number fore multiplyed by the number too equals ate

Unit 25
Sentence 217

how many side does a octagon have asked mr hix eight yelled rose

Unit 25
Sentence 218

you musst multtiply bass times hight to fined the area of a rectangle

Unit 25
Sentence 219

mrs martin said carlos pleaz tell me how many
months names beginn with a vowl

Unit 25
Sentence
220

_____

_____

_____

carlos thinked for a minute and then he said the
answer is three

Unit 25
Sentence
221

_____

_____

_____

thats coreckt said mrs martin the three months
is aprill august and ocktober

Unit 25
Sentence
222

_____

_____

_____

wow kids have there own holliday in japan its called
childrens day and its on may 5

Unit 25
Sentence 223

_____

_____

_____

may 5 is a speshial day in mexico too its called
cinco de mayo

Unit 25
Sentence 224

_____

_____

_____

mothers day and fathers day are holidays inn may
and june

Unit 25
Sentence 225

_____

_____

_____

~~~~~~

shoold them play football baseball or basketbal tommorow at clark park

Unit 26
Sentence 226

_____

_____

_____

~~~~~~

were meating bobby and brad at barker beach at 600 am

Unit 26
Sentence 227

_____

_____

_____

~~~~~~

dont be afrayed said shane there isn't really no goasts in that howse

Unit 26
Sentence 228

_____

_____

_____

Name: _____ Date: _____

chris writed a poem called up in the clowds and he read it alowd to us

_____

_____

_____

sams sister was smileing wen we singed happy birthday to you to her

_____

_____

_____

tara watcht sesame street with the twins untill there parent's comed home

_____

_____

_____

i readed a book called my fathers dragon it taked me
too weaks to read

Unit **26**

Sentence
232

_____

_____

_____

my favorite book is the hobbit said james mine too
said craig

Unit **26**

Sentence
233

_____

_____

_____

us read where the red fern grows it was vary sadd
i liked it anyway

Unit **26**

Sentence
234

_____

_____

_____

there isnt no way to lift this jiant rock said rico its
to heavvy

Unit 27
Sentence
235

_____

_____

_____

lets go to disney world said maria yes that sound fun
said angie

Unit 27
Sentence
236

_____

_____

_____

we drawed picktures of grapes cherrys and other froots
in art class

Unit 27
Sentence
237

_____

_____

_____

who's blue toyota is parked in the wilsons drivewey asked carlton

Unit 27
Sentence
238

_____

_____

_____

we wasn't going to see no movie then greg gived us free tixets

Unit 27
Sentence
239

_____

_____

_____

was you their when the thiefs stealed mrs palmers purse asked officer hall

Unit 27
Sentence
240

_____

_____

_____

Name: _____   Date: _____

Unit 27

Sentence
241

rita runned in the boston marathon last april it was very tireing she finisht

_____

_____

_____

Unit 27

Sentence
242

whose going somewere fun this sumerr asked mrs mackenzie

_____

_____

_____

Unit 27

Sentence
243

we pact are sootcases and leaved for london heathrow airport at 530 am

_____

_____

_____

hanna holded the horses rains loosley in her hands as they troted along

Unit 28
Sentence 244

_____

_____

_____

the kings rein lasted for fourty years and then his neffew becomed king

Unit 28
Sentence 245

_____

_____

_____

uncle fred and ant judy doesn't own a car they live on a iland so they have a bote

Unit 28
Sentence 246

_____

_____

_____

Name: _____ Date: _____

cut the oranges in halfs said curt we need to sqweez
them to make joose

Unit 28
Sentence
247

_____

_____

_____

the wolve's thick cote helpt keep it warm during the
snowey wether

Unit 28
Sentence
248

_____

_____

_____

we shood have swimmed in that lake said stan but it
was freezeing argued andy

Unit 28
Sentence
249

_____

_____

_____

the sine sayed no parking grandpa max parked
their anyway

Unit 28
Sentence 250

_____

_____

_____

a lott of bes was buzing around are picnic tabel we
didn't get stinged

Unit 28
Sentence 251

_____

_____

_____

the man getted down on one nee and askd the women
if she wood mary him

Unit 28
Sentence 252

_____

_____

_____

the old sailer showd us how to tye a strong not in a rope

Unit 29

Sentence
253

_____

_____

_____

the companies owner was in trubble for not payying
his taxs

Unit 29

Sentence
254

_____

_____

_____

nobody never tolled me that their was a shoe sail
at the mall today said clare

Unit 29

Sentence
255

_____

_____

_____

the two boys kites flied over the treetopps and up
hi into the err

Unit 29
Sentence 256

_____

_____

_____

tina troy and keith climed to the top of mount wilson
in june

Unit 29
Sentence 257

_____

_____

_____

dont willys brother play on the mens golf teem at
pacific college

Unit 29
Sentence 258

_____

_____

_____

the guesseds beginned arriveing at pauls pool party at 530 pm

Unit 29
Sentence 259

_____

_____

_____

it has bin a honor to surve this country said the soldyer

Unit 29
Sentence 260

_____

_____

_____

stop yelled officer dugan to the jewlry theif who was trying to excape

Unit 29
Sentence 261

_____

_____

_____

kyles freind just mooved to st paul minnesota last weak

Unit 30
Sentence 262

_____

_____

_____

the clock in the kichen read 300 the one in the liveing room said 342

Unit 30
Sentence 263

_____

_____

_____

the brave night fighted ten mens and reskewed the princess

Unit 30
Sentence 264

_____

_____

_____

nicks mother said its bedtime have you brusht your tooths yet

Unit 30

Sentence 265

_____

_____

_____

we hided behined the oak tree but our friends finded us their

Unit 30

Sentence 266

_____

_____

_____

mike pickd up the two heavyest bag of grocerys and carryed them inside

Unit 30

Sentence 267

_____

_____

_____

the baseball feeld was much muddyer after twelv daze
of rein

_____

_____

_____

mel used a ruler to meazure and draw a strait line that
was elevin inchs long

_____

_____

_____

watt do a banana a skool bus and a egg yoke have in
comon asked mrs foster

_____

_____

_____

Answer Key

Unit 1

Sentence 1: Susan and I saw a movie on Friday at 7:30.

Sentence 2: Mr. Hill has taught at Grant High School for 15 years.

Sentence 3: Have you been to the Grand Canyon in Arizona?

Sentence 4: Those dancers are amazing!

Sentence 5: His best friend is named A.J. Johnson.

Sentence 6: The Warners spent the winter near Whistler Mountain in Canada.

Sentence 7: Our plane will depart from Oklahoma City at 9:45 a.m.

Sentence 8: Is your Spanish teacher named Mrs. Cordova?

Sentence 9: Angie asked if Memorial Day is in April or May.

Unit 2

Sentence 10: Sara, Cindy, and Michelle are going to Africa on May 12, 2012.

Sentence 11: Mr. Miller flew to Miami, Florida, for a business meeting.

Sentence 12: Tito has an appointment with Dr. Stone on Monday, June 5.

Sentence 13: Tanya grows peppers, tomatoes, and squash in her garden.

Sentence 14: Joey was born in Cleveland, Ohio, on August 19, 2004.

Sentence 15: Mrs. Alualu said that it is 4:00 a.m. in Hilo, Hawaii, right now.

Sentence 16: Mark and I played soccer, baseball, and tennis this summer.

Sentence 17: The Olsens bought the house at 368 Main St. on April 12, 2007.

Sentence 18: Should I take a train, plane, or boat from London, England, to Paris, France?

Unit 3

Sentence 19: How many cats does Mrs. Clausen have?

Sentence 20: Mom told us to wash and dry all of the dishes.

Sentence 21: Does Darla have blue, brown, or green eyes?

Sentence 22: Would you like an apple, an orange, or a banana?

Sentence 23: Bree baked a dozen pies for the sale at Pacific Park.

Sentence 24: Clark was excited to see an elephant at the San Diego Zoo.

Sentence 25: We waited over a half an hour for the race to begin.

Sentence 26: Kate, Ella, and Andrew packed boxes of books to sell.

Sentence 27: I ate two eggs, two pancakes, and two slices of bacon for breakfast.

Answer Key (cont.)

Unit 4

Sentence 28: Did you know that a hundred pennies equal one dollar?

Sentence 29: I think those two puppies look like little wolves.

Sentence 30: Amy bought two hats, two scarves, and one pair of gloves.

Sentence 31: There are the same number of days in August, July, and May.

Sentence 32: Is it true that Craig and Sue are both having parties on Saturday?

Sentence 33: The Great Wall of China is one of the most famous landmarks in Asia.

Sentence 34: Did Delia and Deeann dress as witches on Halloween?

Sentence 35: Felicia and her family visited eight beaches this summer.

Sentence 36: We bought two cream pies, six pastries, and a dozen cookies at Boston Bakery.

Unit 5

Sentence 37: Mia's three brothers are named Martin, Max, and Maurice.

Sentence 38: Is it true that Mrs. Bass's new glasses are bright yellow?

Sentence 39: Arturo's baseball team scored nine runs in the fourth inning.

Sentence 40: Her two brothers' wives are both named Alice.

Sentence 41: All of the children's parents watched the game and cheered.

Sentence 42: Charles's chores were to clean the bird's cage and the fish's tank.

Sentence 43: Walter walks Wanda's two dogs every Monday morning at 9:15.

Sentence 44: Mr. Tanner taught us that Rome is the name of Italy's capital city.

Sentence 45: Peter's parents' names are Paul and Penelope Parsons.

Unit 6

Sentence 46: He is the new teacher at Kennedy Junior High School.

Sentence 47: Annie's uncle gave her a new bike for Christmas.

Sentence 48: Are they going to Jill Jones's house for Thanksgiving dinner?

Sentence 49: She watched Jimmy and me play two tennis matches.

Sentence 50: Dee and I have been friends since November 11, 2007.

Sentence 51: We are going to Wrigley Field to watch the Chicago Cubs play.

Sentence 52: P.J. and she are the two best students in Mr. Teal's class.

Sentence 53: My brother, my sister, and I all have brown eyes.

Sentence 54: Martha made two pans of brownies for them and me.

Answer Key (cont.)

Unit 7

Sentence 55: He's going to turn 10 years old on September 2, 2012.

Sentence 56: I'm the best speller in Mrs. Thomas's class.

Sentence 57: Mrs. Ford's the principal at Pine Bluff Elementary School.

Sentence 58: I'll tell Mom and Dad that you'll be late for dinner.

Sentence 59: I've earned twenty more dollars than Rick's earned.

Sentence 60: Didn't you see Sal, Cindy, and Steve at Westlake Mall?

Sentence 61: Is Earth's biggest body of water the Pacific Ocean?

Sentence 62: Mom said you shouldn't eat the soup if it's too hot.

Sentence 63: President Franklin D. Roosevelt's first year in office was 1933.

Unit 8

Sentence 64: Tommy and I run faster than Leah and Josh.

Sentence 65: We were the ones who picked up all your trash yesterday.

Sentence 66: We'll be driving through Arizona, New Mexico, and Texas this summer.

Sentence 67: They left for school at about 7:00 a.m. today.

Sentence 68: Mr. Martin made us sit in our chairs for an hour after class.

Sentence 69: Cassie cried out when the movie's hero fell into the lion's cage.

Sentence 70: Trevor's team stopped at Food Mart to buy drinks and snacks.

Sentence 71: Are we sleeping over at Aunt Deb's house tomorrow night?

Sentence 72: The Wilsons paid P.J. and me to watch their house while they're in Iowa.

Unit 9

Sentence 73: Those are the biggest butterflies I've ever seen!

Sentence 74: I heard that the weather will be much hotter tomorrow.

Sentence 75: Is Tina Tam the smartest person in Mrs. Birch's entire class?

Sentence 76: Claudia and I bought heavier blankets for the winter.

Sentence 77: Do fewer people live in India, China, or the United States?

Sentence 78: The judge said that Kevin's cookies were the tastiest of them all.

Sentence 79: I have been the tallest one of my friends since the third grade.

Sentence 80: They're the funniest guys in the town of Blue Ridge, Virginia.

Sentence 81: She was the happiest one in the house when her team won.

Answer Key *(cont.)*

Unit 10

Sentence 82: Mrs. Mackey, may I sharpen my pencil now?

Sentence 83: No, Andre, you can't play until you finish your homework.

Sentence 84: Wow, those puppies are the tiniest and furriest things ever!

Sentence 85: Yes, we were the ones who went to the concert last night.

Sentence 86: Mom, who ate the cupcake I left on the kitchen table?

Sentence 87: Is he on the Oakview High School boys' volleyball team, too?

Sentence 88: I, too, saw the firefighter save Mrs. Cleary's cat.

Sentence 89: Will you be letting us leave early today, Mr. Timmons?

Sentence 90: Yes, Uncle Nate is the oldest of the seven men in his family.

Unit 11

Sentence 91: "Yes, I'll go if you're going, too," said Alexander.

Sentence 92: "Don't touch that hot oven!" yelled Mrs. Anderson.

Sentence 93: "Who's the current mayor of our town?" asked Mr. Fitz.

Sentence 94: "Are they the thieves who robbed the bank?" asked Officer Kline.

Sentence 95: Bobby said, "No, you can't borrow my brother's bicycle."

Sentence 96: Eli exclaimed, "Wow, that's the best burger I've ever eaten!"

Sentence 97: "Oops!" gasped Vince after tipping over Mrs. Vance's valuable vase.

Sentence 98: Ollie asked "Is Ottawa, Ontario, or Quebec the capital of Canada?"

Sentence 99: Pam pointed at a fin coming out of the ocean and screamed, "Shark!"

Unit 12

Sentence 100: Lily's little sister watched <u>Finding Nemo</u> five times this summer.

Sentence 101: Dr. David sang us a song called "An Apple a Day."

Sentence 102: Donald's dad asked, "Have you read <u>Charlotte's Web</u> by E.B. White?"

Sentence 103: Clarissa's cousin's favorite film is <u>Beauty and the Beast</u>.

Sentence 104: Did Dolly really watch six episodes of <u>Dora the Explorer</u> today?

Sentence 105: Is it true that Aunt Sue's favorite song is "Twist and Shout" by the Beatles?

Sentence 106: "Should we watch <u>Eragon</u>, <u>Star Wars</u>, or <u>Shrek</u>?" asked Alejandro.

Sentence 107: Kim's class read <u>The Lion, the Witch, and the Wardrobe</u> by C.S. Lewis.

Sentence 108: Mia thought that "Flowers" was the best poem in the book <u>Spring Poetry</u>.

Answer Key (cont.)

Unit 13

Sentence 109: Carl's cousin Craig caught the ball and threw it back to Carl.

Sentence 110: "I'm so hungry!" said Harry as he ate a whole pepperoni pizza.

Sentence 111: How many loaves of bread will we need to make forty sandwiches?

Sentence 112: "Can't you see the Atlantic Ocean from here?" asked Nancy.

Sentence 113: Gabriella gave up and said, "It's no use!"

Sentence 114: Lou's sister asked, "Whose blue shoes are those in Lou's room?"

Sentence 115: Our friend Frank is the greatest guitar player in Kern County.

Sentence 116: Two of the main grains grown in Spain are wheat and barley.

Sentence 117: Wally told the waiter, "I'd like an egg and two pieces of toast, please."

Unit 14

Sentence 118: "I never popped any balloons!" swore Sammy to his teacher.

Sentence 119: "Don't we get paid anything for raking those leaves?" asked Art.

Sentence 120: "You can't see anything unless you take off the camera's lens cap," said Paul.

Sentence 121: "Aren't you going to eat anything?" asked Aunt Amelia.

Sentence 122: "Who's not turning in any homework?" demanded Professor Pearl.

Sentence 123: Weren't his jokes any funnier than the other guy's jokes?

Sentence 124: Don't their parents know which movie they're going to see?

Sentence 125: "I haven't ever laughed so hard in my life!" said Grandpa Jack.

Sentence 126: "I am not any good at writing proper paragraphs," admitted Archie Evans.

Unit 15

Sentence 127: Jenny spied on Shirley, and she found out the good news that way.

Sentence 128: Todd wanted to surf, but there weren't any waves at the beach today.

Sentence 129: Tim's parents drove to the supermarket, and they bought some groceries.

Sentence 130: Charles made a hole in the yard, and he buried the treasure there.

Sentence 131: We tried to sit through the whole boring movie, but we couldn't.

Sentence 132: "Don't play with matches, and never leave a candle burning," said Fireman Rick.

Sentence 133: We didn't find any wind, so we couldn't fly our kites.

Sentence 134: We saw four movies yesterday, but we liked only two of them.

Sentence 135: Rex and I made paper airplanes, and we flew them all day long.

Answer Key *(cont.)*

Unit 16

Sentence 136: Kay likes to eat onion rings, but she knows they're not good for her.

Sentence 137: Titus bought a brush, a comb, and some hair gel at Super Mart.

Sentence 138: Does anyone know who's going to visit Henry at the hospital?

Sentence 139: "Ouch!" cried Bonnie when she was stung by a bee.

Sentence 140: They went to Logan Beach, and they swam for an hour.

Sentence 141: The two children said, "Mommy, we want to see an elephant at the zoo."

Sentence 142: The grizzly bear stood up in the river on its hind legs.

Sentence 143: Annabel said, "The best gifts come in little boxes."

Sentence 144: Trent needed two new tires and a pair of windshield wipers for his car.

Unit 17

Sentence 145: "Would you like a lollipop?" asked Lucy. "Yes, I would," said Stan.

Sentence 146: Dad jogged to Hansen Park, but Mom and I rode our bikes there.

Sentence 147: Ty asked, "Can I borrow two dollars?" "I don't have any money," replied Mary.

Sentence 148: The white rabbit hopped over the small fence to get into the garden.

Sentence 149: "Who's been sitting in my chair?" asked Papa Bear.

Sentence 150: The two men were in charge of guarding the queen's jewels.

Sentence 151: Mr. Archer angrily asked, "Whose car is parked in my space?"

Sentence 152: "We've seen rain, snow, and sleet this week. What's next?" asked Ed.

Sentence 153: The princess slept on a pillow made from the feathers of golden geese.

Unit 18

Sentence 154: Ostriches are the heaviest birds. They can weigh over 300 pounds!

Sentence 155: The tiniest bird measures only 2.2 inches long. It's a hummingbird.

Sentence 156: Did you know that a horse can live twice as many years as a squirrel?

Sentence 157: A female deer is called a doe, and a male deer is called a stag.

Sentence 158: A tiger's babies are called cubs, and a bear's are, too.

Sentence 159: Wow, it would take a snail about 30 hours to crawl one mile!

Sentence 160: A tarantula is a hairy spider. It can live for fifteen years.

Sentence 161: Turtles, alligators, and lizards are all reptiles, but frogs aren't.

Sentence 162: Some African elephants can grow to be twelve feet tall. That's huge!

Answer Key *(cont.)*

Unit 19

Sentence 163: Dr. Martin Luther King, Jr. was awarded the Nobel Peace Prize in 1964.

Sentence 164: Yellowstone National Park in Wyoming is home to bears, wolves, and deer.

Sentence 165: In 1927 Charles Lindbergh became the first to fly across the Atlantic Ocean alone.

Sentence 166: "Yankee Doodle" is the official state song of Connecticut.

Sentence 167: The only working diamond mine in North America is in Arkansas.

Sentence 168: Neil named all 50 U.S. state capitals, but Nick forgot that Idaho's is Boise.

Sentence 169: Delaware officially became the first U.S. state on December 7, 1787.

Sentence 170: California, Arizona, and Oklahoma are the states where the most Native Americans live today.

Sentence 171: The world's largest ball of twine can be found in Kansas. It weighs over 18,000 pounds!

Unit 20

Sentence 172: Jupiter and Saturn are the two biggest planets in our solar system.

Sentence 173: The galaxy we live in is called the Milky Way. It contains billions of stars.

Sentence 174: The planet Venus is made up mostly of rock, while Neptune is made mostly of gas.

Sentence 175: There is a belt of rocks called asteroids between Mars and Jupiter.

Sentence 176: A comet is a moving chunk of ice, dust, and rock in space.

Sentence 177: The moon makes no light of its own, but it reflects light from the sun.

Sentence 178: It takes just over 365 days for Earth to revolve around the sun. That's one year.

Sentence 179: The first human to orbit Earth was Yuri Gagarin. He did this on April 12, 1961.

Sentence 180: On July 20, 1969, Neil Armstrong became the first to walk on the moon.

Unit 21

Sentence 181: A penny equals one cent, and a nickel equals five cents.

Sentence 182: Paper money was most likely invented in China.

Sentence 183: The country of Fiji used whales' teeth as money until about 100 years ago.

Sentence 184: Do you know who's on the American $100 bill? It's Benjamin Franklin.

Sentence 185: Ben Franklin was a politician, a writer, an inventor, and a scientist.

Sentence 186: He invented the lightning rod, which helps to keep buildings safe from lightning.

Sentence 187: Our science teacher, Mr. Quail, asked me, "What causes lightning?"

Sentence 188: The blizzard made driving on the town's roads almost impossible.

Sentence 189: A hurricane warning is issued when there are winds over 74 miles per hour.

Answer Key (cont.)

Unit 22

Sentence 190: We learned in health class about food, exercise, and the parts of our bodies.

Sentence 191: The digestive system breaks food down and moves it through your body.

Sentence 192: You were born with 350 bones, but some have grown together. Now you have 206.

Sentence 193: "Are the five senses hearing, sight, smell, taste, and touch?" asked Serena.

Sentence 194: White blood cells in our body help us to fight viruses and bacteria.

Sentence 195: The cerebrum is the part of the brain that controls thinking, speech, and vision.

Sentence 196: Water is very important. It helps us grow, digest food, and get rid of wastes.

Sentence 197: We have three leg bones. They're the femur, the tibia, and the fibula.

Sentence 198: Andy asked, "Does jogging burn more calories than swimming?"

Unit 23

Sentence 199: A photographer spoke to our class yesterday. Her camera was incredible!

Sentence 200: "The three primary colors are red, blue, and yellow," said our art teacher, Mrs. Han.

Sentence 201: They went on a field trip to the J. Paul Getty Museum in Los Angeles.

Sentence 202: "Is it true that this building was designed by your uncle?" asked Avery.

Sentence 203: Carl asked the hotel manager, "Hey, why doesn't this place have a 13th floor?"

Sentence 204: The first elevator was installed in a New York store in 1857. It was powered by steam.

Sentence 205: The world's longest bridge over water is in Louisiana. It's almost 24 miles long!

Sentence 206: "Which explorer is the Hudson Bay named after?" Mr. Alt asked Erin.

Sentence 207: Wow, we spent the morning hiking on a beautiful path called Lizzy's Trail!

Unit 24

Sentence 208: The driest areas on Earth are deserts, and the wettest are rain forests.

Sentence 209: About 67 percent of our world's surface is covered with ocean water.

Sentence 210: Australia's Great Barrier Reef is Earth's largest coral reef.

Sentence 211: Solar power uses energy that comes directly from sunlight.

Sentence 212: The ozone layer protects us from the sun's rays. It is high above Earth.

Sentence 213: Factories and motor vehicles are two of the main sources of air pollution.

Sentence 214: We should take our empty soda cans to the recycling center today.

Sentence 215: Do those companies use recycled paper to make their cereal boxes?

Sentence 216: Mayor Jones is asking for our help in cleaning the city's beaches this Saturday.

Answer Key (cont.)

Unit 25

Sentence 217: The number four multiplied by the number two equals eight.

Sentence 218: "How many sides does an octagon have?" asked Mr. Hix. "Eight!" yelled Rose.

Sentence 219: You must multiply base times height to find the area of a rectangle.

Sentence 220: Mrs. Martin said, "Carlos, please tell me how many months' names begin with a vowel."

Sentence 221: Carlos thought for a minute, and then he said, "The answer is three."

Sentence 222: "That's correct," said Mrs. Martin. "The three months are April, August, and October."

Sentence 223: Wow, kids have their own holiday in Japan! It's called Children's Day, and it's on May 5.

Sentence 224: May 5 is a special day in Mexico, too. It's called Cinco de Mayo.

Sentence 225: Mother's Day and Father's Day are holidays in May and June.

Unit 26

Sentence 226: Should they play football, baseball, or basketball tomorrow at Clark Park?

Sentence 227: We're meeting Bobby and Brad at Barker Beach at 6:00 a.m.

Sentence 228: "Don't be afraid," said Shane. "There aren't really any ghosts in that house."

Sentence 229: Chris wrote a poem called "Up in the Clouds," and he read it aloud to us.

Sentence 230: Sam's sister was smiling when we sang "Happy Birthday to You" to her.

Sentence 231: Tara watched <u>Sesame Street</u> with the twins until their parents came home.

Sentence 232: I read a book called <u>My Father's Dragon</u>. It took me two weeks to read.

Sentence 233: "My favorite book is <u>The Hobbit,</u>" said James. "Mine, too," said Craig.

Sentence 234: We read <u>Where the Red Fern Grows</u>. It was very sad, but I liked it anyway.

Unit 27

Sentence 235: "There isn't any way to lift this giant rock," said Rico. "It's too heavy."

Sentence 236: "Let's go to Disney World," said Maria. "Yes, that sounds fun," said Angie.

Sentence 237: We drew pictures of grapes, cherries, and other fruits in art class.

Sentence 238: "Whose blue Toyota is parked in the Wilsons' driveway?" asked Carlton.

Sentence 239: We weren't going to see a movie, but then Greg gave us free tickets.

Sentence 240: "Were you there when the thieves stole Mrs. Palmer's purse?" asked Officer Hall.

Sentence 241: Rita ran in the Boston Marathon last April. It was very tiring, but she finished.

Sentence 242: "Who's going somewhere fun this summer?" asked Mrs. Mackenzie.

Sentence 243: We packed our suitcases and left for London Heathrow Airport at 5:30 a.m.

Answer Key (cont.)

Unit 28

Sentence 244: Hanna held the horse's reins loosely in her hands as they trotted along.

Sentence 245: The king's reign lasted for forty years, and then his nephew became king.

Sentence 246: Uncle Fred and Aunt Judy don't own a car. They live on an island, so they have a boat.

Sentence 247: "Cut the oranges in halves," said Curt. "We need to squeeze them to make juice."

Sentence 248: The wolf's thick coat helped keep it warm during the snowy weather.

Sentence 249: "We should have swam in that lake," said Stan. "But it was freezing," argued Andy.

Sentence 250: The sign said "No Parking," but Grandpa Max parked there anyway.

Sentence 251: A lot of bees were buzzing around our picnic table, but we didn't get stung.

Sentence 252: The man got down on one knee and asked the woman if she would marry him.

Unit 29

Sentence 253: The old sailor showed us how to tie a strong knot in a rope.

Sentence 254: The company's owner was in trouble for not paying his taxes.

Sentence 255: "Nobody ever told me that there was a shoe sale at the mall today," said Clare.

Sentence 256: The two boys' kites flew over the treetops and up high into the air.

Sentence 257: Tina, Troy, and Keith climbed to the top of Mount Wilson in June.

Sentence 258: Doesn't Willy's brother play on the men's golf team at Pacific College?

Sentence 259: The guests began arriving at Paul's pool party at 5:30 p.m.

Sentence 260: "It has been an honor to serve this country," said the soldier.

Sentence 261: "Stop!" yelled Officer Dugan to the jewelry thief who was trying to escape.

Unit 30

Sentence 262: Kyle's friend just moved to St. Paul, Minnesota, last week.

Sentence 263: The clock in the kitchen read 3:00, but the one in the living room said 3:42.

Sentence 264: The brave knight fought ten men and rescued the princess.

Sentence 265: Nick's mother said, "It's bedtime. Have you brushed your teeth yet?"

Sentence 266: We hid behind the oak tree, but our friends found us there.

Sentence 267: Mike picked up the two heaviest bags of groceries and carried them inside.

Sentence 268: The baseball field was much muddier after twelve days of rain.

Sentence 269: Mel used a ruler to measure and draw a straight line that was eleven inches long.

Sentence 270: "What do a banana, a school bus, and an egg yolk have in common?" asked Mrs. Foster.